Beasts

A Christmas Poem With Music

illustrated by Ruth Sanderson

A GOLDEN BOOK • NEW YORK
Western Publishing Company, Inc. Racine, Wisconsin 53404

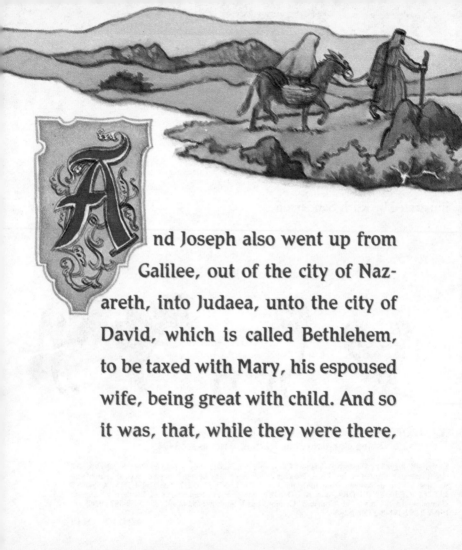

And Joseph also went up from Galilee, out of the city of Nazareth, into Judaea, unto the city of David, which is called Bethlehem, to be taxed with Mary, his espoused wife, being great with child. And so it was, that, while they were there,

THE FRIENDLY BEASTS

THE FRIENDLY

the days were accomplished that she should be delivered. And she brought forth her firstborn son, and wrapped him in swaddling clothes, and laid him in a manger, because there was no room for them in the inn.

Luke 2: 4–7

JESUS our brother, kind and good,
Was humbly born in a stable rude,
And the friendly beasts around Him stood;
Jesus our brother, kind and good.

"I," said the donkey, shaggy and brown,
"I carried His mother up hill and down,
  I carried her safely to Bethlehem town;
I," said the donkey, shaggy and brown.

"I," said the cow, all white and red,
"I gave Him my manger for His bed,

I gave Him my hay to pillow His head;
I," said the cow, all white and red.

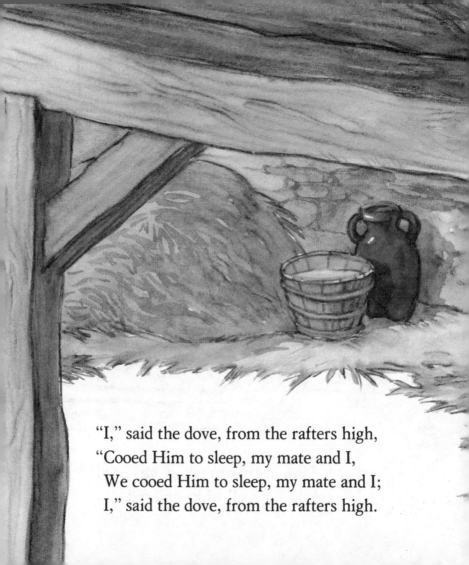

"I," said the dove, from the rafters high,
"Cooed Him to sleep, my mate and I,
    We cooed Him to sleep, my mate and I;
    I," said the dove, from the rafters high.

"I," said the rooster, with a shining eye,
"I crowed the news up to the sky,
  When the sun arose, I crowed to the sky;
  I," said the rooster, with a shining eye.

"I," said the sheep, with the curly horn,
"I gave Him my wool for His blanket warm;
He wore my coat on Christmas morn.
I," said the sheep with the curly horn.

"I," said the camel, all yellow and black,
"Over the desert upon my back,

I brought Him a gift in the Wise Men's pack;
I," said the camel, all yellow and black.

So every beast, by some good spell,
In the stable dark, was glad to tell,
Of the gift he gave Emmanuel,
The gift he gave Emmanuel.

THE FRIENDLY BEASTS

English *Music Adapted by Marie Donnaruma*

Je - sus our bro - ther, kind and good,

Was humb - ly born in a sta - ble rude,

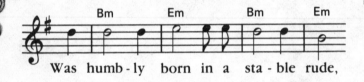

And the friend - ly beasts a - round Him stood;

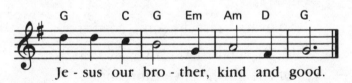

Je - sus our bro - ther, kind and good.

"I," said the donkey, shaggy and brown,
"I carried His mother up hill and down,
I carried her safely to Bethlehem town;
I," said the donkey, shaggy and brown.

"I," said the cow, all white and red,
"I gave Him my manger for His bed,
I gave Him my hay to pillow His head;
I," said the cow, all white and red.

"I," said the dove, from the rafters high,
"Cooed Him to sleep, my mate and I,
We cooed Him to sleep, my mate and I;
I," said the dove, from the rafters high.

"I," said the rooster, with a shining eye,
"I crowed the news up to the sky,
When the sun arose, I crowed to the sky;
I," said the rooster, with a shining eye.

"I," said the sheep, with the curly horn,
"I gave Him my wool for His blanket warm;
He wore my coat on Christmas morn.
I," said the sheep, with the curly horn.

"I," said the camel, all yellow and black,
"Over the desert upon my back,
I brought Him a gift in the Wise Men's pack;
I," said the camel, all yellow and black.

So every beast, by some good spell,
In the stable dark, was glad to tell,
Of the gift he gave Emmanuel,
The gift he gave Emmanuel.